Third Eye of the Inner Light

Other books by Matt Bialer

POETRY

Radius (Les Editions du Zaporogue) 2012

Already Here (Black Coffee Press 2012

Ark (Black Coffee Press) 2012

Black Powder (Black Coffee Press) 2013

Bridge (Leaky Boot Press) 2013

Tell Them What I Saw (PS Publishing) 2014

Ascent (JournalStone) 2014

He Walks on all Fours (Dynatox Ministries) 2015

Kings of Men (Dynatox Ministries) 2015

Wing of Light (Les Editions du Zaporogue) 2015

Frequencies (Leaky Boot Press) 2015

Formation (Weirdo Magnet) 2016

Distant Shores (Villipede) 2016

Wonder Weavers (JournalStone) 2016

The Valley of the Eight (Leaky Boot Press) 2017

PHOTOGRAPHY

More Than You Know (Les Editons du Zaporogue) 2011

A Moment's Notice (Les Editions du Zaporogue) 2016

PAINTING

Shadowbrook (Les Editions du Zaporogue)) 2012

Third Eye of the Inner Light

an epic poem

Matt Bialer

LEAKY BOOT PRESS

Third Eye of the Inner Light
by Matt Bialer

First published in 2018 by
Leaky Boot Press
http://www.leakyboot.com

ISBN: 978-1-909849-66-2

Third Eye of
the Inner Light

The Spirit Molecule calls
It calls

In room 631

She leaps up

Ready to answer

Ready to answer

In her session

We see many
Of the sure signs

Of a mystical experience

The suspension

Of the boundaries

Of time and space

The ecstatic nature

Of the encounter

Her own divinity

Brief
But intensely felt

The Spirit Molecule calls
It calls

In room 631

She leaps up

Ready to answer

Ready to answer

In room 631

University of New Mexico
School of Medicine

Albuquerque

Tenured associate professor

The Spirit Molecule calls
It calls

25 Years of research

Effects of psychedelics

Or hallucinogenic drugs
On humans

In particular
Effects of N, N-dimethyltryptamine

Or DMT

Short acting

Powerful psychedelic

The Spirit Molecule

60 volunteers

400 injections

The Spirit Molecule calls
It calls

In room 631

She leaps up

Ready to answer

Ready to answer

The suspension

Of the boundaries

Of time and space

The ecstatic nature

Of the encounter

Her own divinity

Descartes says

"I think, therefore I am"

But he needs

A source for these thoughts

A source

From where
In the brain

Might thought arise?

He proposes

The pineal gland

Only singleton organ

Of the brain

A source for these thoughts

A source

Ebb and flow

Of cerebrospinal fluid

Through the ventricles

Perfectly suited

For corresponding movement

Of thoughts

The pineal gland

Descartes believes

Human imagination

A spiritual phenomenon

Made possible

By our divine nature

What we share

With God

Our thought

Expressions of

Proof of the existence

Of our soul

Believes the pineal gland

Plays an essential role

The seat of the soul

Third Eye

Becomes visible

In the developing fetus

At seven weeks

Or 49 days after conception

Same moment

One can clearly see

The first indication

Of male or female gender

Before this time

Sex of the fetus

Unknown

Pineal gland

And male or female gender

Appear at the same time

The Spirit Molecule calls
It calls

In room 631

She leaps up

Ready to answer

Ready to answer

In her session

We see many

Of the sure signs

Of a mystical experience

The suspension

Of the boundaries

Of time and space

The ecstatic nature

Of the encounter

Her own divinity

Brief
But intensely felt

The Spirit Molecule calls
It calls

Third Eye

Not actually

A part of the brain

Develops from
Specialized tissues

In roof
Of fetal mouth

Migrates
To the center

Of the brain

Close to
Emotional

And sensory centers

Relay station

For transmission
Of sense data

In brain sites

Involved in their

Registration
And interpretation

Electrical

And chemical impulses

That begin
In the eyes

And ears

Must pass
Through perceptual hubs

Visual and auditory colliculi

Before we experience them

In our minds

As sights
And sounds

Pineal gland

Third Eye

Hangs directly
Over these colliculi

Separated only
By a narrow channel

Of cerebrospinal fluid

The pineal

Possesses melatonin

Profound psychedelic properties

Vehicle by which

The pineal

Acts on our spiritual lives

Melatonin

A tryptamine

Like DMT

The Spirit Molecule

Already within us

The Spirit Molecule

Third Eye

The Spirit Molecule calls
It calls

In room 631

What they say

They see

When they travel

To the other realms

Machine Elves

Stick Men

Hyperspace Jesters

Clowns

Jimjam

Discarnate Beings

Folding Rooms

Spirit Guides

The Visitors

Aliens

Central Light

Arch Angels

Everything that is

Has been

Can be

Will be

Never was

Never could be

What they say

They see

When they travel

To the other realms

The Spirit Molecule calls
It calls

In room 631

She leaps up

Ready to answer

Ready to answer

From where
In the brain

Might thought arise?

Third Eye

25 Years of research

Effects of psychedelics

Or hallucinogenic drugs
On humans

In particular
Effects of N, N–dimethyltryptamine

Or DMT

Short acting

Powerful psychedelic

The Spirit Molecule

60 volunteers

400 injections

I spend
A lot of time

Procuring permits

To manufacture
Illegal drug

Apply for research funding

University will
Supply some

But I need more

More

National Institute on Drug Abuse

Call a Mr. S
At NIDA

We want to help
Call Mr. C at DEA

Can Mr. C
Manufacture some human grade DMT

For my project?

High score from NIDA
For my grant application

DEA receives information
From the FDA

Protocol sound enough
For the FDA

To approve "in principle"

Schedule permit

Diversion Control
Blocked the permit

Who's Diversion Control?
I've never heard of them

We want to help
Call Mr. C at DEA

Can Mr. C
Manufacture some human grade DMT

For my project?

Months of run around

May I begin the DMT study?

Your hold has been removed

You have verbal approval

University won't accept that

I need a letter

I need a letter

An e-mail

Finally it comes

Finally

Your hold has been removed

We want to help
Call Mr. C at DEA

Can Mr. C
Manufacture some human grade DMT

For my project?

The Spirit Molecule calls
It calls

In room 631

She leaps up

Ready to answer

Ready to answer

In our volunteers

A full dose of intravenous DMT

Almost instantly

Causes profound psychedelic visions

Visions

The mind separates

From the body

Separates

Overwhelming emotions

DMT doses

0.2, 0.3 and 0.4 mg/kg

Effects begin

Within seconds

Of finishing

30 second drug infusion

Volunteers

Fully engaged

With their psychedelic realms

Visions

By the time

I finish clearing

The intravenous line

With sterile saline

15 seconds later

Peak of DMT trip

About 2 minutes in

Feel like they're
Coming down at 5 minutes

Not able to talk
12 to 15 minutes

After infusion

Remain moderately
Intoxicated

Most feel normal
At 30 minutes

Lower dose
Of DMT

.01 and 0.05 mg/kg

Generally not
Psychedelic experiences

But still produce
Some psychological effects

Emotional
Physical

Some sensitive volunteers

Significant psychedelic
And physical responses

To even low doses

Some of them
Drop out

Don't like the intensity

Of low 0.05 mg/kg dose

Others excused

Blood pressure too high

Worry about heart attack

At eight times the dose

With these higher amounts

Heart rate
And pulse

Leap from 70 beats
Per minute

To 100

Some even to 150

Blood pressure
Also jumps

From about 110/70

To average of 145/100

Pupil diameter doubles
From 4 millimeters

To nearly 8

Body temperatures rise

Of all biological factors
We monitor

The only one
That does not increase

Pineal gland hormone melatonin

Astonishing

Again brings home

The mystique

Of the spirit gland

The spirit gland

May be

Outside administered DMT

Not powerful enough

To stimulate gland

Another possibility

Exogenous DMT

Did stimulate the pineal

To make more of

Its own
Endogenous DMT

But our method
Of measuring

DMT in the blood

Not able
To distinguish

Between the two sources

Of the Spirit Molecule

Registration
And interpretation

Electrical

And chemical impulses

That begin
In the eyes

And ears

Must pass
Through perceptual hubs

Visual and auditory colliculi

Before we experience them

In our minds

As sights
And sounds

Pineal gland

Third Eye

Hangs directly
Over these colliculi

Separated only
By a narrow channel

Of cerebrospinal fluid

The pineal

Possesses melatonin

Profound psychedelic properties

Vehicle by which

The pineal

Acts on our spiritual lives

Melatonin

A tryptamine

Like DMT

The Spirit Molecule

Already within us

The Spirit Molecule

Third Eye

The Spirit Molecule calls
It calls

In room 631

We want to help
Call Mr. C at DEA

Can Mr. C
Manufacture some human grade DMT

For my project?

Diversion Control
Blocked the permit

Who's Diversion Control?
I've never heard of them

We want to help
Call Mr. C at DEA

Your hold has been removed

You have verbal approval

University won't accept that

I need a letter

I need a letter

An e-mail

Finally it comes

Finally

Your hold has been removed

The Spirit Molecule
It calls

It calls

In room 631

We see many

Of the sure signs

Of a mystical experience

The suspension

Of the boundaries

Of time and space

The ecstatic nature

Of the encounter

The initial moments

Of the first non-blind high dose

Of DMT

Overwhelms almost everyone

Overwhelms

An intense rush

Sudden turbulent movement

Feeling of urgency

Haste

Swift violent shakes

Blurt out

Here we go!

Some compare
Feeling to a freight train

Standing

On a mountain summit

Face in the high wind

High wind

Vibrations

Coursing through them

Powerful energy pulse

I don't think I can stay in my skin

High wind

My body's gone!

It's gone!

Deep breathing

What they say

They see

When they travel

To the other realms

Machine Elves

Stick Men

Hyperspace Jesters

Clowns

Jimjam

Discarnate Beings

Folding Rooms

Spirit Guides

The Visitors

Aliens

Central Light

Arch Angels

Everything that is

Has been

Can be

Will be

Never was

Never could be

What they say

They see

When they travel

To the other realms

The Spirit Molecule calls
It calls

In room 631

She leaps up

Ready to answer

Ready to answer

From where
In the brain

Might thought arise?

Third Eye

Phone beeps

My daughter Alexa

Everyone calls Lexi

Petit

Thin

27 years old

Tattoos of chrysanthemums

On her shoulders

Entire ribcage

Autumnal flower

Bright fuchsia

Swirling red and green

Pop off her skin

In China

A symbol of Taoist simplicity
And perfection

Tranquility

Completeness

And abundance

Following the harvest

Worked in a tattoo parlor

Taught by a master

Now makes her own clothes

Chrysanthemum Fashions

Sells online

Vintage pastel print dresses

Shirts

Sweaters

Scarves

Often with patterns

Of the flower itself

Husband Paul

A brewer

Nexus Brewery

Owner's favorite Star Trek movie

The one where

Captain Kirk and Picard

Get pulled into the Nexus

Heavenly place

Where everything is perfect

Pulled into the Nexus

An establishment

That rivals
Captain Kirk's nirvana

Nexus Silver Taproom

Cream Ale

Equinox

Chocolate Porter

To Boldly Gose

Hi Lexi

Hi Dad

How was Max's first week
Of school?

Their son
4 years old

That's what I'm calling about

Started a new school
This year

Class is in hot basement

One of the youngest

Showing aggressive behavior
In school

And at home

Only towards grown-ups
Never kids

His teachers piss me off

They're young and inexperienced

Something happened in school
To trigger this

But they're labeling him
Trying to convince me

He has issues

Issues caused by
Them probably

It's me against them

They're against me

Ok, Ok
Do you think maybe he does?

I don't know
You're the shrink

But I'm not
An OT

Occupational Therapist

Did you ask your mother?

She told me
To talk to you

That's funny

My ex
An addiction psychiatrist

Last night
I asked him

To clean up his train toy

He started throwing pieces at me

Last weekend
He was terrified at the circus

Holding his ears

Says the clown's
Giant bow tie scared him

And the face paint

I think it's getting worse

The teachers think it's weird
He doesn't like ice cream

I said so what?

So what?

What's wrong with Max, Dad?

I don't know Lexie

Is he autistic?

It could be nothing

Or it could be many things

APHD
ODD
Autism
SPA

We don't know

He needs to get tested

Let me get a good recommendation

We're really worried Dad

I'll find someone

Pulled into the Nexus

Autumnal flower

Bright fuchsia

Swirling red and green

A symbol of Taoist simplicity
And perfection

Tranquility

Completeness

And abundance

Following the harvest

What they say

They see

When they travel

To the other realms

Machine Elves

Fractal Elves

Self-transforming elf machines

Dream Wizards

Elementals

Aliens: Insectoids like Praying Mantises

Reptilians

Ghosts

Discarnate Entities

Morphos

Hyperspace Jesters

Circus Ringleaders

Flirty Fairies

Mother Goddess

Glass Chrysanthemums

Arch Angels

Everything that is

Has been

Can be

Will be

Never was

Never could be

What they say

They see

When they travel

To the other realms

The Spirit Molecule calls
It calls

In room 631

She leaps up

Ready to answer

Ready to answer

From where
In the brain

Might thought arise?

Third Eye

One of my volunteers

A woman named Betty

40 years old

Divorced twice

A hot stone massage therapist

Use of smooth, flat
Heated stones

Placed on specific
Parts of your body

Basalt river rocks
Typically used

Have become smooth
Over time

From river currents

Retain heat

110–130 degrees

Generally placed
Along both sides

Of the spine

Palms of the hand

Legs

Between toes

Always tells me

You should try it sometime
I won't charge you

I will sometime
And of course I'll pay

I mean it

Where were you
When I was getting divorced?

Betty's married again

An auto mechanic

Sharp sense of humor

Belly laugh

Some problems
With current husband

*More depressed
Than I am*

That's a problem

Has done
Psychedelic drugs

About 20 times
In her life

Finds them
Very mind-opening

Manages first
Low does screening very well

The Spirit Molecule calls
It calls

In room 631

She leaps up

Ready to answer

Ready to answer

From where
In the brain

Might thought arise?

Third Eye

Get pulled into the Nexus

Heavenly place

Where everything is perfect

Pulled into the Nexus

Next day's high dose

Kaleidoscopic patterns

Something Mayan

Islamist

Aztec

Beautiful colors
Pink cobwebs

Elongation of light

It's beautiful Robert

Just beautiful

Have you ever tried this?

I'm not at liberty so say

Tremendous
Intricate

Geometric colors

Like being
An inch

From a color television

Pink cobwebs

Elongation of light

Blue of a desert sky

But on another planet

Colors more intense

Afterwards

Talks about her marriage

Husband in therapy

Tells him
To be more honest with her

More honest

Tells her she's getting fat

Sexual turn off

Maybe there's more
Going on than that

More going on

Autumnal flower

Bright fuchsia

Swirling red and green

A symbol of Taoist simplicity
And perfection

Tranquility

Completeness

And abundance

Following the harvest

Have become smooth
Over time

From river currents

An intense rush

Sudden turbulent movement

Feeling of urgency

Haste

Swift violent shakes

Blurt out

Here we go!

Some compare
Feeling to a freight train

Standing

On a mountain summit

Face in the high wind

High wind

Vibrations

Coursing through them

Powerful energy pulse

I don't think I can stay in my skin

High wind

My body's gone!

It's gone!

Deep breathing

Another injection

There are these dolls

19th century outfits

Life-sized

Women in corsets

Big breasts and butts

Very skinny waists

Whirling around Betty

Tip toes

Men in top hats

Riding two seater bicycles

Merry-go-rounds

Women with red circles

Painted on their cheeks

Calliope music

A clown

Red nose

White face

Colorful baggy pants

Flower squirting water

Talking

Laughing

But no sound

Another encounter
With clowns

I had been

Hearing about
Quite some time

From the volunteers

Clowns

In this other realm

What do you make
Of that

I ask her later

I don't know Robert

But no more circuses for me!

She laughs

What is the Spirit Molecule
Trying to tell us?

What is it
Trying to tell us?

What they say

They see

When they travel

To the other realms

Machine Elves

Stick Men

Hyperspace Jesters

Clowns

Jimjam

Discarnate Beings

Folding Rooms

Everything that is

Has been

Can be

Will be

Never was

Never could be

What they say

They see

When they travel

To the other realms

The Spirit Molecule calls
It calls

In room 631

She leaps up

Ready to answer

Ready to answer

From where
In the brain

Might thought arise?

Third Eye

Another volunteer

Sadie

21 years old

Next to youngest

Short

Close cropped hair

Muscular

Nose ring

Androgynous

Intelligent

Sharp sense of humor

Doesn't always
Take care of herself

Older nurses
Want to feed her

Bathe her

Suffered in relationships

Parents divorced
At 2 years old

Mother struggled
To raise her

Own demons
To deal with

Left her alone
With stepfather

Raped her
When she was 16

Distrustful
Of people

Post-Traumatic Stress Disorder

Flashbacks
Of the rape

Years of therapy
Failed romantic relationships

That's life I guess

That's life

What do you hope
To get out of these sessions Sadie?

I don't know
That something's better, I guess

Out there, I mean

Asks that
We not speak to her

While she is
Under the influence

Enjoy the full trip

Screening low dose
Of DMT

Mild and pleasant

Pineal gland

Third Eye

Hangs directly
Over these colliculi

Separated only
By a narrow channel

Of cerebrospinal fluid

The pineal

Possesses melatonin

Profound psychedelic properties

Vehicle by which

The pineal

Acts on our spiritual lives

Melatonin

A tryptamine

Like DMT

The Spirit Molecule

Already within us

The Spirit Molecule

Third Eye

The Spirit Molecule calls
It calls

In room 631

We want to help
Call Mr. C at DEA

Can Mr. C
Manufacture some human grade DMT

For my project?

Diversion Control
Blocked the permit

Who's Diversion Control?
I've never heard of them

We want to help
Call Mr. C at DEA

Your hold has been removed

You have verbal approval

University won't accept that

I need a letter

I need a letter

An e-mail

Finally it comes

Finally

Your hold has been removed

The Spirit Molecule
It calls

It calls

In room 631

We see many

Of the sure signs

Of a mystical experience

The suspension

Of the boundaries

Of time and space

The ecstatic nature

Of the encounter

Next day
Non blind

0.4 mg/kg high dose

Something takes her hand

Yanks her

Seems to say

Let go

Blue cob webs

Elongation of light

Let go

Out of body

In a maze

Moving fast

Kaleidoscopic

Flower patterns

It seems so real

Realer than real

A circus side show

A look like jokers

Performing for her

Wear funny looking bells

On their hats

Big noses

Feels like

They could turn on her

Turn on her

Not completely friendly

The Spirit Molecule
It calls

It calls

In room 631

We see many

Of the sure signs

Of a mystical experience

The suspension

Of the boundaries

Of time and space

The ecstatic nature

Of the encounter

The initial moments

Of the first non-blind high dose

Of DMT

Overwhelms almost everyone

Overwhelms

An intense rush

Sudden turbulent movement

Feeling of urgency

Haste

Swift violent shakes

Blurt out

Here we go!

Some compare
Feeling to a freight train

Standing

On a mountain summit

Face in the high wind

High wind

Vibrations

Coursing through them

Powerful energy pulse

I don't think I can stay in my skin

High wind

My body's gone!

It's gone!

Deep breathing

Next day

Sadie comes back

It doesn't make any sense

What happened to me

Impossible to prepare for

Good mood

You're a Psychonaut

A what?

A Psychonaut

I like the sound of that

Psychonaut

Waits table
At a local restaurant

Met a woman

Whom she really likes

She feels like
The DMT has freed her

The Spirit Molecule
Has freed her

Helping her let go

Let go of the rape

Feels a lot freer

It seems so real

Realer than real

Tremendous
Intricate

Geometric colors

Like being
An inch

From a color television

Pink cobwebs

Elongation of light

Have become smooth
Over time

From river currents

Her last dose

She sees visitors

Visitors, I ask?

Elves

Don't know what else
To call them

Many visitors

Jovial

Laughing

Smiling at me

Like they're glad to see me

Glad I came back

Yes, I feel like
I was here before

We're glad you're back

You're back

The Spirit Molecule calls
It calls

In room 631

She leaps up

Ready to answer

Ready to answer

In her session

We see many
Of the sure signs

Of a mystical experience

The suspension

Of the boundaries

Of time and space

The ecstatic nature

Of the encounter

Her own divinity

Brief
But intensely felt

The Spirit Molecule calls
It calls

In room 631

She leaps up

Ready to answer

Ready to answer

My doorbell rings

My house
Desert mountain view

It's my son Brian

Two years older
Than Lexi

Single

Works for a
Virtual Reality Company

The Chasm

Hyper Reality

Whole body

Fully immersive
VR experience

Surprises
At every turn

With your family
Friends

Inside the action

One second

You're standing

On solid ground

The next

Stepping
Deep into darkness

Deep into darkness

Beholding
Unimaginable beauty

Of fending off danger
From another realm

Did you see it?

Did you feel it?

What's next?

Unmatched realism

Takes you

Entirely out of

Your own world

And into another

The Chasm

Realer Than Real

Not just visually

But physically

Emotionally

Can enter
Unexplored worlds

Filled with
Immersive and

Entertaining adventure

Virtual Reality

VR you can feel

Go ahead
Reach out

Touch a real wall

A real rail

Then feel a breeze
Across your face

And the experience begins

Brian

Tall

Samurai ponytail
Or semi bun

Top of his head

Loose, long, dark hair
In the back

Are you ready Dad?

Ready for today's session?

I'm not sure

This whole thing
Is like I'm going to die

Well you are going to die

But not in the foreseeable future

Come on
Mom's been a sport about it

He calls mine Dadbot

Hers is Mombot

Going to create
A doll

Artificial intelligence

Version of me

Dr. Robert Strand

Preserve me forever

Dadbot

Technology

That allows people

To have conversations
With characters

Who don't exist

In the fictional world

Like Buzz Lightyear

Or because
They're dead

I'm not dead Brian

But you will be one day

And this is a long term project

And Lexi and Paul
And me

And Max

And whoever

Can still have you

Dadbot

A chatbot

That emulates me

Already has
91,970 words

He's recorded

Put into neural network

Chatbot

Draws from corpus
Of human speech

Communicate
In my distinctive manner

Convey
At least some

Of my personality

Dadbot

This is too weird

I'm going to keep him
On my book shelf

Now that's creepy

Right now
It's just a crapbot Dad

Records me

Where I was born

Where I went to school

Girlfriends

Childhood memories

Where I met his mother

My work
With psychedelic drugs

How do you feel
About your work?

I have mixed feelings

It's fascinating

But I don't know
If it's doing any good

Helping people

And I hate the bureaucracy

We want to help
Call Mr. C at DEA

Can Mr. C
Manufacture some human grade DMT

For my project?

Diversion Control
Blocked the permit

Who's Diversion Control?
I've never heard of them

We want to help
Call Mr. C at DEA

Your hold has been removed

You have verbal approval

We see many

Of the sure signs

Of a mystical experience

The suspension

Of the boundaries

Of time and space

The ecstatic nature

Of the encounter

The initial moments

Of the first non-blind high dose

Of DMT

Overwhelms almost everyone

Overwhelms

An intense rush

Sudden turbulent movement

Feeling of urgency

Haste

Swift violent shakes

Blurt out

Here we go!

Some compare
Feeling to a freight train

Standing

On a mountain summit

Face in the high wind

High wind

Vibrations

Coursing through them

Powerful energy pulse

I don't think I can stay in my skin

High wind

My body's gone!

It's gone!

Deep breathing

Elves

Don't know what else
To call them

Many visitors

Jovial

Laughing

Smiling at me

Like they're glad to see me

Glad I came back

Yes, I feel like
I was here before

We're glad you're back

You're back

The Spirit Molecule calls
It calls

In room 631

That's how I feel
About the Chasm

It's fun
But so what?

VR can help people

Help people

Train surgeons

Train soldiers

It could help
A kid like Max

This is popcorn

A crapbot

Bots get good

When their code

Split apart

Like the forks

Of a giant maze

User inputs

Trigger bot response

Each leading

To a fresh slate

Of user inputs

Until the program
Has thousands of lines

Navigational commands
Ping-pong

User around
Conversational structure

Becomes increasingly
Byzantine

Snippets of speech

We anticipate
A user might say

Written elaborately

Drawing on deep banks
Of phrases

And synonyms

Governed by
Boolean logic

Rules combined
To form meta-rules

Called intents

To interpret
More complete user utterances

Intents can be
Generated automatically

Powerful machines
Learning engines

Offered by Google,
Facebook, Pull String

Face recognition

This is ridiculous Brian

Dad, it will take months

Maybe years

But my flimsy
How are you sequence

Has taught me
How to create

The first atoms
Of the conversational universe

Childhood

University

Mom

Patients

Songs and Jokes

It will be smarter than you Dad

Smarter than you

And funnier

What is that sound?

Take your proton blaster

And save the world

You're inside The Chasm
With your entire

Mind and body

Immersed in virtual world

Where reality

And imagination

Mix in breathtaking

Hyper-realistic experience

The Chasm

One second

You're standing

On solid ground

The next

Stepping
Deep into darkness

Deep into darkness

Beholding
Unimaginable beauty

Of fending off danger
From another realm

Did you see it?

Did you feel it?

The Chasm

Realer Than Real

What is the Spirit Molecule
Trying to tell us?

What is it
Trying to tell us?

What they say

They see

When they travel

To the other realms

Machine Elves

Stick Men

Hyperspace Jesters

Clowns

Jimjam

Discarnate Beings

Folding Rooms

Everything that is

Has been

Can be

Will be

Never was

Never could be

What they say

They see

When they travel

To the other realms

The Spirit Molecule calls
It calls

In room 631

She leaps up

Ready to answer

Ready to answer

From where
In the brain

Might thought arise?

Third Eye

It becomes apparent
That many of the volunteers

Experience similar realms
The same beings

Not clearly related
To the thoughts, feelings

And bodies
Of our participants

Suggests freestanding
Independent levels

Of existence

About which
We are at most

Only dimly aware

These reports

Challenge our world view

Are these dreams?

Hallucinations?

Or is it real?

Real

Where are these places?

Inside or out?

Are these
Other dimensions?

Elves

I don't know what else
To call them

Many visitors

Jovial

Laughs

Smiling at me

Like they're glad to see me

Glad I came back

Yes, I feel like
I was here before

We're glad
You're back

You're back

We begin to
Identify these realms

Experiences

Beings

And chart them out

The Hyperspace Jester

I meet
With all of the time

All of the time

Has more knowledge
About the world

Than I do

Correctly uses words
I have to look up later

Not sure if it is speaking
Or telepathy

What gets me

We talk about things

I've never heard of before

Never heard of

When we first met

He told me about

Shiva and Shakti

Had heard the name Shiva

But never heard
The name Shakti

In my life

Didn't know
Their story

I looked it up

Divine masculine
Divine feminine

Twin names

Which I also
Never heard of

He brought this up
Out of nowhere

Very romantic

Flirts

Claims to be
My soul mate

In love with me

Always guides me

We call him

The Hyperspace Jester

In "love"

With many volunteers

Might be
Playing with them

Relay station

For transmission
Of sense data

In brain sites

Involved in their

Registration
And interpretation

Electrical

And chemical impulses

That begin
In their eyes

And ears

And pass
Through perceptual hubs

Visual and auditory colliculi

Before we experience them

In our minds

And sights
And sounds

Pineal gland

Third Eye

Hangs directly
Over these colliculi

Separated only
By a narrow channel

Of cerebrospinal fluid

The pineal

Possesses melatonin

Powerful psychedelic properties

Vehicle by which

The pineal

Acts on our spiritual lives

Melatonin

A tryptamine

Like DMT

The Spirit Molecule

Already within us

The Spirit Molecule

Third Eye

The Spirit Molecule calls

It calls

In room 631

Call a Mr. S
At NIDA

We want to help
Call Mr. C at DEA

Can Mr. C
Manufacture some human grade DMT

For my project?

High score from NIDA
For my grant application

DEA receives information
From the FDA

To approve "in principle"

Schedule permit

Diversion Control
Blocked the permit

Who's Diversion Control?
I've never heard of them

Months of run around

May I begin the DMT study?

Your hold has been removed

You have verbal approval

I need a letter

I need a letter

An e-mail

Finally it comes

Finally

Your hold has been removed

We want to help

We want to help

Tattoos of chrysanthemums

On her shoulders

Entire ribcage

Autumnal flower

Bright fuchsia

Swirling red and green

Pops off her skin

In China

A symbol of Taoist simplicity

And perfection

Tranquility

Completeness

And abundance

Following the harvest

Basalt river rocks

Typically used

Have become smooth
Over time

From river current

Last weekend
He was terrified at the circus

Holding his ears

Says the clown's
Giant bow tie scared him

And the face paint

Holding his ears

You're a psychonaut

A what?

A psychonaut

I like the sound of that

Psychonaut

We are bombarded
With billions of signals

Every second

All of which

Except for smell

Enter through
The thalamus

The thalamus,
Hypothalamus and pineal

Part of a large structure

Called the diencephalon

Structures

Relay station

Switchboard

From the brain

To the rest of the body

Bombarded
With billions of signals

All of which

Except for smell

Enters through
The thalamus

Filters these things

Down to what is essential

Before passing them
On to the cortex regions

Where our higher functioning
Occurs

When we consume
These psychedelics

Thalamus stops
Filtering the signals

Rather than getting
A very clean filtered

Slice of existence

We are getting it all

Getting it all

Filtering mechanism

Switched off

Serotonin temporarily loses
Its repressive control

Over conscious state

Bombarded
With billions of signals

Filter switched off

We begin to
Identify these realms

Experiences

Beings

And chart them out

Breakthrough

Beyond life of death

Beyond time or space

Or known dimensions

Inherently synesthetic

Ultra-sharp edges

Highly polished surfaces

Endlessly morphing

And fractalizing details

A sense of extremely
High energy

And vibration

As well
As frantic activity

All one

Feels oddly familiar

Maybe where we
Were before birth

And will return
After death

Everything that is

Has been

Can be

Will be

Never was

Never could be

A Chrysanthemum

Or Glass Chrysanthemum

A gigantic

Often spinning

Fractal flower

With a domelike appearance

That frequently

Either welcomes

Or blocks access

To Breakthrough Hyperspace

Folding Rooms

Multidimensional spaces

That certain Hyperspace beings

Often entangle

Enmesh

And overlap travelers in

Actually seem to fold over

And in on themselves

And the observers viscerally

Reaching behind

And around one

With their architecture

Hyperspace

The place you go

After Breakthrough

Can be any place

And time

Imaginable

Where the impossible

Can really happen

Extreme geometric

Explosions of color

Sound

Emotions

Feelings of
Being hyper real

Realer than real

Clowns

Seen commonly

All different types

Or sizes

Not known

If they're benevolent

Hyperspace Jester

Harlequins

Or Fools

Truly resemble

Medieval jesters

Not silly

Or foolish

In any way

Hyper intelligent

Male versions

Of the Flirty Fairies

Try to show off

And show you things

Objects

Hyperspace tarot cards

Similar to Machine Elves

Maybe the same species

Machine Elves

The most common beings

Of Hyperspace

Fractal elves

Self-transforming elf machines

Often reported
Being seen

By our volunteers

Even more than clowns

At about one minute

Or two of the DMT trip

May burst through

A chrysanthemum mandala

And find a whole bunch
Of entities

Waiting on the other side

The other side

One second

You're standing

On solid ground

The next

Stepping
Deep into darkness

Deep into darkness

Beholding
Unimaginable beauty

Find a whole bunch
Of entities

Waiting on the other side

The other side

How wonderful

That you're here

You come so rarely

We're so delighted to see you

Jeweled

Self-dribbling basketballs

Stop in front of you

And vibrate

Jump into your body

And jump back out again

Watch what we're doing!

Watch!

Making objects

With their voices

Singing structures

Into existence

Offer things to you

Look at this!

Look at this!

Realize

What is being shown

To you
Is impossible

Impossible

Some sort of
Glowing Faberge egg

But looks
Otherworldly

And toys

That seem
To be alive

Sing other toys
Into existence

Elf gifts
Everywhere

And they're shouting

Do it!

Do it!

The initial moments

Of the first non-blind high dose

Of DMT

Overwhelms almost everyone

Overwhelms

An intense rush

Sudden turbulent movement

Feeling of urgency

Haste

Swift violent shakes

Blurt out

Here we go!

Some compare
Feeling to a freight train

Standing

On a mountain summit

Face in the high wind

High wind

Vibrations

Coursing through them

Powerful energy pulse

I don't think I can stay in my skin

High wind

My body's gone!

It's gone!

Deep breathing

Elves

Don't know what else
To call them

I hear
From Lexi

They're seeing
An OT

Occupational Therapist

I found a good recommendation

Trying to figure out
What is going on with Max

He's getting worse Dad

Worse

Enjoys listening
To music loud

TV loud

But when it comes
To loud toilet

Loud hair dryer

He freaks

Like he is in pain

Hold his ears

Cries

Afraid

He started
Taking his clothing off

When he gets home
From school

On days
Of no school

In his underwear
All of the time

What's wrong Max?

What's wrong?

Started complaining

About underwear

Socks

Shoes too tight

Too close

Or just uncomfortable
In general

I keep going
To Target

Get him
Different types

And sized

To comfort him

But it's all
A big struggle

Getting ready for school

Paul and I
Are exhausted

What do they think it is?

Could be autism

ADHD

But I don't it
Because he can focus

On things

When it is
The right environment

ODD

But they think
It is maybe SPD

Sensory Processing Disorder

Full panel test done

Waiting for results

I have a question Dad

Why does he
Act this way with us

But not with you
Or Brian

Or kids at school

Or even the doctor's office

Sits there
Happy and quiet

Maybe he's better
One on one

Or a new environment
Calms him down

With you guys
He's an angel

With us
It's rough

Sounds like SPD
But I'm not a specialist

And SPD
And ADHD symptoms

Can overlap

Some kids
Can have both

Hypersensitivity to sound
And sights

Can be both

They'll diagnose it
And get a treatment going

Let me know
About the test results

I will

How is Dadbot?

Oh don't ask

He wants to come over
And have me relive

My earliest memories

I think it is so cool

Mombot is coming along too

How's the clothing business?

Good

I'm doing
A pop up store

This holiday season

Do you want me
To help out?

I can on weekends

Sure
Thanks Dad

It's fun
And I know nothing

About clothing

We know that Dad
That's why you'll be

Working the register

The Spirit Molecule calls
It calls

In room 631

She leaps up

Ready to answer

Ready to answer

In her session

We see many
Of the sure signs

Of a mystical experience

The suspension

Of the boundaries

Of time and space

The ecstatic nature

Of the encounter

Her own divinity

Brief
But intensely felt

The Spirit Molecule calls
It calls

In room 631

She leaps up

Ready to answer

Ready to answer

In room 631

University of New Mexico
School of Medicine

Albuquerque

Tenured associate professor

The Spirit Molecule calls
It calls

25 Years of research

Effects of psychedelics

Or hallucinogenic drugs
On humans

In particular
Effects of N, N-dimethyltryptamine

Or DMT

Short acting

Powerful psychedelic

The Spirit Molecule

60 volunteers

400 injections

The Spirit Molecule calls
It calls

In room 631

She leaps up

Ready to answer

Ready to answer

The suspension

Of the boundaries

Of time and space

The ecstatic nature

Of the encounter

Her own divinity

Descartes says

"I think, therefore I am"

But he needs

A source for these thoughts

A source

From where
In the brain

Might thought arise?

Third Eye

Where does DMT

Take us by the hand

And lead us to?

Where?

We chart

And map

The Spirit Molecule's territory

Chart

And map

Evan

A first dose

Response study volunteer

A plumber

Within 2 minutes

First non-blind low dose

Spirals

Of what look like

DNA

Red and green

Another volunteer
Rosie

Owns an art gallery

Also sees
The familiar double helix pattern

On her double blind
0.4 mg/kg dose

Dropping back
Into tubes

Like protozoa

The inside
Of a cell

Twirling

And spiraling

Gelatin

Another volunteer
Sam

Also sees
These DNA-like spirals

Made up
Of glowing bright cubes

Red
Yellow
Blue

Release my soul's energy

My soul's energy

Loses his body

Spirals
All around him

Like things
He's seen at Chaco Canyon

Maybe that was DNA

Ancients knew that

Carlos

42 years old

Documentary filmmaker

Worked with us
In many

Of our pilot studies

Sort out doses

And combinations

Low dose
mg/kg

Visuals

Soft
And geometric

Looks like
An alphabet

But not English

Something old

Runes

Arabic

Feels like
Information

Embedded in it

Embedded in it

Data

Not just random

Alphabet-like figures

Panels
With cut out shapes

Rounded

Hieroglyphics

Not painted on

But cut out

Through which

He sees bright colors

Red
Green
Violet

Clarissa

27 years old

Works for
Software company

Travel apps

Also sees
Visual transformation

Of language
And numbers

One of the most
Experienced volunteers

Over 200 LSD trips

Smoked DMT as well

Thousands of words

Or DNA

Everywhere

Blue amoebic shapes

Pulsating

There are lots of them!

Meaning

Or symbols

They mean something

Some kind of
Core of reality

Core of reality

Where all meaning
Is stored

Breaking through

A membrane

Into a feeling

Of meaning

And certainty

Maybe because
I love computers

The raw bits
Of reality

A lot more
Than only ones

And zeros

Proceeds
Into a white room

Folds into
And back onto itself

Folding room

Convertible Cadillac
Drives by

Full of clowns

Colored wigs

Pompoms

Making faces
At her

White face paint

Red mouths

Shiny teeth

In the room

That is growing

Light

And space

Cubes
Stacked with icons

On the surfaces

Logos of consciousness

Other volunteers

Find themselves

In rooms

Some that fold up

Playrooms

Nurseries

Holding space

Made especially for them

Full of meaning
And depth

One says
It's a nursery

No babies

But there were cribs

With different animals

Not familiar

Vibrant

Cartoon-like people
In the room

Clowns

Hyperspace Jesters

Machine Elves

Another volunteer

Doug

A window washer

Who likes mushrooms

46 years old

Beholds elements
Of unseen world

Informational language aspect

Nursery/playroom theme

There's a door

Nothing to walk through

Either over here

Dark

Or over there

Images

You can't do anything
With them

Major hieroglyphics

That turn
Into a room

Strange toys

Glowing Faberge eggs

I was a kind

I'm with the elves, I think

Tell me

They're glad I came back

Yes maybe I am

5 of them

Scream at me

To do it!

Do it!

We're glad you're back!

Another volunteer

Led to
Some sort of apartment

Betty

Teacher at trapeze school

28 years old

Blind 0.2 mg/kg dose

A living space

From the future

Laughs
At how weird

That is

Living quarters

Bright neon pink

Orange and yellow

Counters

Molded out of the walls

Almost
Like it's alive

Furniture
Is breathing

Breathing

May I begin the DMT study?

Your hold has been removed

You have verbal approval

I need a letter

I need a letter

An e-mail

Finally it comes

Finally

Your hold has been removed

We want to help

We want to help

Tattoos of chrysanthemums

On her shoulders

Entire ribcage

Autumnal flower

Bright fuchsia

Swirling red and green

Pops off her skin

In China

A symbol of Taoist simplicity

And perfection

Tranquility

Completeness

And abundance

Following the harvest

Basalt river rocks

Typically used

Have become smooth
Over time

From river current

Did you feel it?

The Chasm

Realer Than Real

What is the Spirit Molecule
Trying to tell us?

What is it
Trying to tell us?

What they say

They see

When they travel

To the other realms

Machine Elves

Stick Men

Hyperspace Jesters

Straw Men

Angels

Dream Wizards

Elementals

Aliens

Clowns

Jimjam

Discarnate Beings

Folding Rooms

Everything that is

Has been

Can be

Will be

Never was

Never could be

What they say

They see

When they travel

To the other realms

The Spirit Molecule calls
It calls

In room 631

She leaps up

Ready to answer

Ready to answer

From where
In the brain

Might thought arise?

Third Eye

My doorbell rings

It's my son Brian

Tall

Samurai ponytail
Or semi bun

Top of his head

Loose, long, dark hair
In the back

Are you ready Dad?

Ready for today's session?

Not really

Oh come on Dad

Dadbot's getting smarter

He'll be better than you

Dadbot

Going to create
A doll

Artificial intelligence

Preserve me forever

Dadbot

Technology

That allows people

To have conversations
With characters

Who don't exist

In the fictional world

Like Buzz Lightyear

Or because
They're dead

I'm not dead Brian

Nobody lives forever

Not even the great psychiatrist

Dadbot

A chatbot

That emulates me

Already has
92,356 words

He's recorded

Put into neural network

Chatbot

Draws from corpus
Of human speech

Communicate
In my distinctive manner

Convey
At least some

Of my personality

Dadbot

Records me

Where I was born

Girlfriends

Education

My work
With psychedelic drugs

How do you feel
About your work?

I have mixed feelings

It's fascinating

But I don't know
If it's doing any good

Helping people

And I hate the bureaucracy

We want to help
Call Mr. C at DEA

Can Mr. C
Manufacture some human grade DMT

For my project?

Diversion Control
Blocked the permit

Who's Diversion Control?
I've never heard of them

We want to help
Call Mr. C at DEA

Your hold has been removed

You have verbal approval

We see many

Of the sure signs

Of a mystical experience

The suspension

Of the boundaries

Of time and space

The ecstatic nature

Of the encounter

The initial moments

Of the first non-blind high dose

Of DMT

Overwhelms almost everyone

Overwhelms

An intense rush

Sudden turbulent movement

Feeling of urgency

Haste

Swift violent shakes

Blurt out

Here we go!

Some compare
Feeling to a freight train

Standing

On a mountain summit

Face in the high wind

High wind

Vibrations

Coursing through them

Powerful energy pulse

I don't think I can stay in my skin

High wind

My body's gone!

It's gone!

Deep breathing

Elves

Don't know what else
To call them

Many visitors

Jovial

Laughing

Smiling at me

Like they're glad to see me

Glad I came back

Yes, I feel like
I was here before

We're glad you're back

You're back

The Spirit Molecule calls
It calls

In room 631

Dozens of sessions

Lasting an hour

His audio recorder runs

It runs

Used to explore caves

When I was young

With some friends

We embraced the darkness

Embrace the darkness

Took a job during college

Loading ice blocks

Into railroad box cars

For the hell of it

Wanted to be

Ripped for the ladies

And I was

Embrace the darkness

Voice recognition

Processing power

Dadbot

A chatbot

That emulates

Not a children's toy

But a very real man

Me

Dadbot

Let's do more childhood memories Dad

Being in my father's arms

In a crowded office

And reaching up

To touch an overhead light

Touch the light

And scalding myself

It's when I said

My first word

After I touched the light

My father said "hot"

And I repeated "ott"

I was less than a year old

Wow Dad

Grandma and Grandpa
Confirmed the memory

Tell me more Dad

Going to the circus

We arrive

In a winding hallway

My father

Points to a humanless

Automated organ

Playing a song

Steam boiler sound

Trumpets, French horns

Cornets, tubas

White and black keys

Automatically

Go up and down

Humanless

Touch the light

Continue

Walk down the hall

A clown appears

Looming over me

Just a few feet

From my face

Smiles

Says hi

Continues to stare at me

Arms out stretched

I just stand there in silence

Robert, you say hello?

My dad requests

I continue

To take it in

Patterns of clown's greasepaint

He's a man

Underneath that

Has to be

Points to a humanless

Automated organ

Playing a song

Steam boiler sound

Trumpets, French horns

Cornets, tubas

White and black keys

Automatically

Go up and down

Humanless

He's a man

Underneath that

Has to be

Aren't you going to say hello?

Both the clown

And my father

Give up on me

Give up

Humanless

Aren't you going to say hello?

Embrace the darkness

Touch the light

After the session

Dad, I'm actively looking

For a new job

I want to do something

More cool

With VR

More beneficial

Did you see it?

Did you feel it?

What's next?

Unmatched realism

Takes you

Entirely out of

Your own world

And into another

The Chasm

Realer Than Real

Not just visually

But physically

Emotionally

Can enter
Unexplored worlds

Filled with
Immersive and

Entertaining adventure

Virtual Reality

VR you can feel

Go ahead
Reach out

Touch a real wall

A real rail

Then feel a breeze

Across your face

And the experience begins

What kind of place Brian?

I don't know

But there are tons
Of places

Pushing the envelope
With the technology

It can help people Dad

Not just give

People a thrill

One second

You're standing

On solid ground

The next

Stepping
Deep into darkness

Deep into darkness

He's a man

Underneath that

Has to be

Points to a humanless

Automated organ

Playing a song

Steam boiler sound

Trumpets, French horns

Cornets, tubas

White and black keys

Automatically

Go up and down

Humanless

He's a man

Underneath that

Has to be

Touch the light

Aren't you going to say hello?

The Spirit Molecule calls
It calls

In room 631

She leaps up

Ready to answer

Ready to answer

In her session

We see many
Of the sure signs

Of a mystical experience

The suspension

Of the boundaries

Of time and space

The ecstatic nature

Of the encounter

Her own divinity

Brief
But intensely felt

Descartes says

"I think, therefore I am"

But he needs

A source for these thoughts

A source

From where
In the brain

Might thought arise?

He proposes

The pineal gland

Only singleton organ

Of the brain

A source for these thoughts

A source

Ebb and flow

Of cerebrospinal fluid

Through the ventricles

Perfectly suited

For corresponding movement

Of thoughts

The pineal gland

Descartes believes

Human imagination

A spiritual phenomenon

Made possible

By our divine nature

What we share

With God

Our thought

Expressions of

Proof of the existence

Of our soul

Believes the pineal gland

Plays an essential role

The seat of the soul

Third Eye

Becomes visible

In the developing fetus

At seven weeks

Or 49 days after conception

Same moment

The first indication

Of male or female gender

Before this time

Sex of the fetus

Unknown

Pineal gland

And male and female gender

Appear at the same time

The Spirit Molecule calls
It calls

In room 631

She leaps up

Ready to answer

Ready to answer

A part time graduate student

Jonathan

Of Jonny

As he likes to be called

Joins my small team

Long hair

Slender

Shaggy beard

An unrepentant Deadhead

Fan of stoner rock

I hand over to him

Much of the initial screening

Of prospective DMT volunteers

Returns calls

Asks the first series

Of questions

In terms of suitability

Explains the studies

In which the caller
Might participate

Meets with me
To discuss various personnel

Whether to move people

Forward in the screening process

If we have additional questions

Jonny follows up

Takes him a few months

To get up to speed

On what the studies are

Properties of the drugs

What I require

The Federal Government's protocol

We want to help
Call Mr. C at DEA

Can Mr. C
Manufacture some human grade DMT

For my project?

Diversion Control
Blocked the permit

Who's Diversion Control?
I've never heard of them

We want to help
Call Mr. C at DEA

Your hold has been removed

You have verbal approval

University won't accept that

I need a letter

I need a letter

An e-mail

Finally it comes

Finally

Your hold has been removed

Latecomer
To psychedelic field

Very enthusiastic

Almost childishly so

Loves the project

Always eager

Finds the volunteers fascinating

Spends time
With them

Attends meetings
And conferences

Well known
Psychedelic research scientists

But I have concerns
About Jonny

As earnest as he is

Concerns

One of the volunteers
Invites him

To her house
To take drugs

And he can't
Pass up the opportunity

I tell him
I'm concerned

It's not appropriate

Not appropriate

Relax man

Robert, you've been doing this
For so long

I'm way behind

I'm educating myself

There's nothing improper

I tell him not
To do it

But I don't prohibit it

Also concerned
Because we're giving

Higher doses

Trips or experiences
More intense

Wherever they go

Some of the volunteers

Having NDEs

Near Death Experiences

Perhaps the pineal

Releases DMT

Or something like that

When someone's dying

Or maybe

Just maybe

This other realm

Is real

And the barriers

Have come down

Come down

Third Eye

Barriers

Have come down

These reports

Challenge our world view

Are these dreams?

Hallucinations?

Or is it real?

Real

Where are these places?

Inside or out?

Are these
Other dimensions?

Elves

I don't know what else
To call them

Many visitors

Jovial

Laughs

Smiling at me

Like they're glad to see me

Glad I came back

Yes, I feel like
I was here before

We're glad
You're back

You're back

We begin to
Identify these realms

Experiences

Beings

And chart them out

The one where

Captain Kirk and Picard

Get pulled into the Nexus

Heavenly place

Where everything is perfect

Pulled into the Nexus

Basalt river rocks
Typically used

Have become smooth
Over time

From river currents

You're a Psychonaut

A what?

A Psychonaut

I like the sound of that

Psychonaut

You're inside The Chasm
With your entire

Mind and body

Immersed in virtual world

Where reality

And imagination

Mix in breathtaking

Hyper-realistic experience

The Chasm

One second

You're standing

On solid ground

The next

Stepping
Deep into darkness

Deep into darkness

Beholding
Unimaginable beauty

Of fending off danger
From another realm

Did you see it?

Did you feel it?

The Chasm

Realer Than Real

What is the Spirit Molecule
Trying to tell us?

What is it
Trying to tell us?

What they say

They see

When they travel

To the other realms

Machine Elves

Stick Men

Hyperspace Jesters

Clowns

Jimjam

Discarnate Beings

Folding Rooms

Spirit Guides

The Glass Chrysanthemum

The Visitors

Aliens

Central Light

Arch Angels

Everything that is

Has been

Can be

Will be

Never was

Never could be

What they say

They see

When they travel

To the other realms

Andrea

41 years old

Married to a contractor

Two kids

Out of the house

Lives in a
More rural

Part of the county

Medical social worker

Treats drug abusing professionals

Aware that it is

Kind of funny
That I'm in this study

Appreciates our
Strict concern

For confidentiality

And anonymity

Takes psychedelics

3 to 4 times a year

Around 30 times
In general

Volunteers
For the DMT project

Because she's heard
About how powerful

The drug is

I'm nervously curious

I want to learn
About myself

Andrea's low
Non-blind dose

Produces
Stronger than average effects

Sees lots of spirals

Green and red DNA

That was a rush!

I warn her

That tomorrow's high dose

Will hit her
Like a freight train

I'm up for it

Next morning

Few pleasantries

Right down

To business

Administer
The high dose

Lays perfectly still
For 25 minutes

Her body
Makes small jerk

That's it!

In a very

Enchanting place

Don't want

To leave it

Don't want to

Transitions

Are completions

Completions

How she is

Who she is

Channel of light

Off to right

Follow it

Bright and pulsating

Sound

Almost like music

For cello

Doesn't recognize it

Feel very small

Large beings

In the tunnel

Large beings

Sense of great speed

Everything else

Unimportant

Flashing, overwhelming light

So much more

Real than life

'

More real

Than life

Overwhelming light

A tunnel
On the left

Left and right tunnels

Gremlins

Small faces mostly

Wings and tails

Bright teeth

Tries to ignore them

Larger beings here

To sustain

And support her

Sustain

And support her

This is their realm

They are the good ones

Gremlins are not

Tall beings

Loving

Smiling

Serene

Feels separation

From her body

Knows

This is the death realm

Always heard

About the light tunnel

Thought it would

Be in front of her

Not on both sides

And joined in front

The Spirit Molecule calls
It calls

In room 631

She leaps up

Ready to answer

Ready to answer

The suspension

Of the boundaries

Of time and space

The ecstatic nature

Of the encounter

Her own divinity

Descartes says

"I think, therefore I am"

But he needs

A source for these thoughts

A source

From where
In the brain

Might thought arise?

Third Eye

Where does DMT

Take us by the hand

And lead us to?

Where?

We chart

And map

The Spirit Molecule's territory

Chart

And map

A sense of extremely
High energy

And vibration

As well
As frantic activity

All one

Feels oddly familiar

Maybe where we
Were before birth

And will return
After death

Everything that is

Has been

Can be

Will be

Never was

Never could be

A Chrysanthemum

A gigantic

Often spinning

Fractal flower

With a domelike appearance

That frequently

Either welcomes

Or blocks access

To Breakthrough Hyperspace

Folding Rooms

Multidimensional spaces

That certain Hyperspace beings

Often entangle

Enmesh

And overlap travelers in

Actually seem to fold over

And in on themselves

And the observers viscerally

Reaching behind

And around one

With their architecture

Hyperspace

The place you go

After Breakthrough

Can be any place

And time

Imaginable

Where the impossible

Can really happen

Extreme geometric

Explosions of color

Sound

Emotions

Feelings of
Being hyper real

Realer than real

Clowns

Seen commonly

All different types

Or sizes

Not known

If they're benevolent

Hyperspace Jester

Harlequins

Or Fools

Truly resemble

Medieval jesters

Not silly

Or foolish

In any way

Hyper intelligent

Male versions

Of the Flirty Fairies

Try to show off

And show you things

Objects

Hyperspace tarot cards

Similar to Machine Elves

Maybe the same species

Machine Elves

The most common beings

Of Hyperspace

Fractal elves

Self-transforming elf machines

Often reported
Being seen

By our volunteers

Even more than clowns

At about one minute

Or two of the DMT trip

One may
Burst through

A chrysanthemum mandala

And find a whole bunch
Of entities

Waiting on the other side

The other side

One second

You're standing

On solid ground

The next

Stepping
Deep into darkness

Deep into darkness

Beholding
Unimaginable beauty

Find a whole bunch
Of entities

Waiting on the other side

The other side

How wonderful

That you're here

You come so rarely

We're so delighted to see you

Jeweled

Self-dribbling basketballs

Stop in front of you

And vibrate

Jump into your body

And jump back out again

Watch what we're doing

Watch!

Always heard

About the light tunnel

Thought it would

Be in front of her

Not on both sides

And joined in the front

Amazing

That DMT

Is in the body

In the body

It's there for

A reason

For a reason

I know

What dying is

I know

No words

Bodies

Or sounds

There to limit things

Deep space

White with stars

It's alive

It's the aliveness

I thought I could see

Light down below

The world's light

Like a little flap

Was lifted

Miguel

47 years old

From Hispanic

And northern Mexican-Indian lineage

A curandero

Native healer

Shaman

Married
For 20 years

Two grown sons

Fulltime software engineer

Graduate
University of New Mexico

Well versed
In mind altering substances

Particularly
From herbs and plants

Taken psychedelics

Too many times to count

But many hundreds of times

Interested
In altered states of consciousness

Done lots of peyote

Mescaline

Mushrooms

Datura Stramonium

Known as jimsonweed

Originated in Mexico

Is not
Expecting much from study

Curious

But skeptical
That any white man

Can produce
A better drug

Nothing personal doc

But we've doing this for thousands of years

And we don't need labs

Part of me
Really wants to

Prove him wrong

With some "white man" drugs

Oh boy

Morning of
Non blind low dose

Arrives two hours early

Wants to be prepared

Still skeptical, mind you

This is will be a trip
Around the block

Nothing more

His low dose experience

Relatively mild

And eventless

Until he starts shaking

Shaking

After the injection

Start as tremors

Then body shakes

I hate this part

I always shake

Maybe it's fear Miguel

Nothing wrong with that

You know

I'm fine

This is nothing

Looks frightened
To me

We give him
Some cracker snacks

Don't worry about me

See you tomorrow

Next day's injection

Goes smoothly

At 12 minutes

Laughs loudly

Oh boy!

There is no spiritual value

What do you mean?

I was wondering

What is this?

Then it comes to me

This is the drug

This is what it does

Too much to process

Like trying to
Listen to music

That is too loud

Don't know what is going on

What is going on?

Did he die?

Spirit death

My Spirit was destroyed

What do you mean
By spirit?

Do you mean self-image?

Your identity?

We can argue
About terms

It's the unborn

And the undying

I see myself

Who I am

At a fundamental level

Remember Miguel

This is only half a big dose

Wow, that's amazing

You're getting it now

Let yourself go

Two mornings later

Miguel's 0.4 mg/kg high dose

Sweating

Shaking

When I enter the room

It's body fear

It's nothing

Let's proceed

Begins chanting

As I administer drug

Stops

Let's out big sigh

At 2 minutes

Chants some more

More softly

3 and ½ minutes

At twelve minutes

Please remove
My eye shades

I met myself

As the Creator

Creator of?

The Creator
Of All

I always say

You can still be
An atheist

Until 0.4

Sound of
The entire universe

Entire universe

A hum

Pervasive

Overwhelming

A man

Lying in a hospital room

Naked

A person
Each side of him

One female

One male

Something

Wrong with him

Wrong

There to get better

Hospital

A healing center

But what's wrong
With him?

He's dead

Stress from DMT

That's me dead

He is healed

More than healed

Reborn

Cured from death

Becomes
Center of the universe

Becomes
More and more solid

Moves toward
Everyday presence

Witness
The creation

Of the universe

From the fundamental
Mental energy

To a vibration

To all things

Recreates the hospital

And the room

Witness
The creation

Of the universe

We want to help
Call Mr. C at DEA

Can Mr. C
Manufacture some human grade DMT

For my project?

High score from NIDA
For my grant application

DEA receives information
From the FDA

To approve "in principle"

Schedule permit

Diversion Control
Blocked the permit

Who's Diversion Control?
I've never heard of them

Months of run around

May I begin the DMT study?

Your hold has been removed

You have verbal approval

I need a letter

I need a letter

An e-mail

Finally it comes

Finally

Your hold has been removed

We want to help

We want to help

Tattoos of chrysanthemums

On her shoulders

Entire ribcage

Autumnal flower

Bright fuchsia

Swirling red and green

Pops off her skin

In China

A symbol of Taoist simplicity

And perfection

Tranquility

Completeness

And abundance

Following the harvest

Basalt river rocks

Typically used

Have become smooth
Over time

From river current

Last weekend
He was terrified at the circus

Holding his ears

Says the clown's
Giant bow tie scared him

And the face paint

Holding his ears

You're a psychonaut

A what?

A psychonaut

I like the sound of that

Psychonaut

We are bombarded
With billions of signals

Every second

All of which

Except for smell

Enter through
The thalamus

The thalamus,
Hypothalamus and pineal

Part of a large structure

Called the diencephalon

Structures

Relay station

Switchboard

From the brain

To the rest of the body

Bombarded
With billions of signals

All of which

Except for smell

Enters through
The thalamus

Filters these things

Down to what is essential

Before passing them
On to the cortex regions

Where our higher functioning
Occurs

When we consume
These psychedelics

Thalamus stops
Filtering the signals

Rather than getting
A very clean filtered

Slice of existence

We are getting it all

Getting it all

Filtering mechanism

Switched off

Serotonin temporarily loses
Its repressive control

Over conscious state

Bombarded
With billions of signals

Filter switched off

We begin to
Identify these realms

Experiences

Beings

And chart them out

Breakthrough

Beyond life of death

Beyond time or space

Or known dimensions

Inherently synesthetic

Ultra-sharp edges

Highly polished surfaces

Endlessly morphing

And fractalizing details

A sense of extremely
High energy

And vibration

As well
As frantic activity

All one

Feels oddly familiar

Maybe where we
Were before birth

And will return
After death

Everything that is

Has been

Can be

Will be

Never was

Never could be

A Chrysanthemum

A gigantic

Often spinning

Fractal flower

With a domelike appearance

That frequently

Either welcomes

Or blocks access

To Breakthrough Hyperspace

Folding Rooms

Multidimensional spaces

That certain Hyperspace beings

Often entangle

Enmesh

And overlap travelers in

Actually seem to fold over

And in on themselves

And the observers viscerally

Reaching behind

And around one

With their architecture

Hyperspace

The place you go

After Breakthrough

Can be any place

And time

Imaginable

Where the impossible

Can really happen

Extreme geometric

Explosions of color

Sound

Emotions

Feelings of
Being hyper real

Realer than real

I help Lexi

Set up pop shop

Empty retail space

Cottonwood Mall

About 30 merchants

Pottery

Fashion

Including Chrysanthemum Fashions

Handmade guitars

Hand carved music boxes

Custom made chocolates

Landscape paintings

Photography

Christmas tree ornaments

Wreaths

It's good for business Dad

Physical shops

A great way

To add human element

To the brand

Engage customers offline

Many shoppers

Still want

To see and touch items
Before they make purchases

To see and touch

Temporary offline store

Allows shoppers
Who may have been hesitant

About purchasing online

To test out

And learn more

About certain products

Last minute holiday shoppers

More likely to
Head to brick and mortar stores

And the mall

To pick up gifts

Rather than browse

For products online

Allows me to
Personally get to know

My customers

Build stronger relationships

Which in turn

Drives customer royalty

Plus I can see what they like

And why

And I can mark things down

Sell overstock

It's a win-win Dad

And this booth pays for itself

To see and touch

Max has been diagnosed
With SPD

Sensory Processing Disorder

I hate that word Dad

Disorder

Therapy not really working

You have to give it time Lexi

Like money
In a piggy bank

Well the piggy bank's
Gonna break

Been very hyper

Can't sit still

Says the clown's
Giant bow tie scared him

And the face paint

I think it's getting worse

The teachers think it's weird
He doesn't like ice cream

I said so what?

So what?

Can't concentrate
Very well

Loves rough textures

Oh really?

Likes the lava rocks

In our front yard

First thing he goes to

Can't stop rubbing them

Basalt river rocks
Typically used

Have become smooth
Over time

From river currents

Retain heat

110-130 degrees

Generally placed
Along both sides

Of the spine

Palms of the hand

Legs

Between toes

Always tells me

You should try it sometime
I won't charge you

First thing he goes to

Still a pill with us

Left him with our neighbor
And their kids

Was afraid
Of what we'd hear

When we picked him up

Said he was
A perfect little angel

Perfect little angel

Noises set him off

He does
All of these weird things

Whenever
There is a loud sudden noise

Or groups of people

We were
Rushing to an appointment

Hustling along
A crowded sidewalk

Kept dragging his feet

Traffic loud

Smell of exhaust

A kid on a bike
Blowing a whistle

And a storefront

Bursting with bright vegetables

Flowers

Stopped in his tracks

Long loud scream

Agony and frustration

Everyone turned around

And glared

Later I asked him

Why he screamed

Why he screamed

He didn't know

Couldn't control the impulse

Terrified of playground swings

Walking barefoot
In the grass

Last weekend
He was terrified at the circus

Holding his ears

Says the clown's
Giant bow tie scared him

And the face paint

Holding his ears

You're a psychonaut

A what?

A psychonaut

I like the sound of that

Psychonaut

We are bombarded
With billions of signals

Every second

Diagnosed
With SPD

By occupational therapist

Trained in SI

Sensory Integration

We are bombarded
With billions of signals

Every second

Sensory Integration

Process by which

Information from our senses

Touch

Sight

Hearing

Taste

Smell

As well as balance

Interpreted by the brain

So that we correspond

Appropriately to our environment

A child with

Good SI

Automatically filters

The important

From the unimportant stimuli

As they make their way

Through the world

For children

With SPD

Information

Reaching the senses

Often feels

Like an assault

Of competing stimuli

Three children

Telling you

Conflicting stories

About who had the toy

The telephone is ringing

Suddenly smell the cake
Burning in the oven

Did I mention

The itchy rash
On your legs?

For others

Outside stimuli dulled

As if a shade

Has been pulled over

Muting sights, sounds,
Touch

These children

Crave extra stimulation

To arouse themselves

Most children
With SPD

Display elements
Of both extremes

Sensory overload

And sensory deprivation

A child playing

In a sandbox

Can ignore
The sweat

Trickling down his face

Because he loves the sandbox

A breeze to cool off
A little

A child

With SPD

Cannot ignore anything

Cannot ignore

The sweat distracts

And the wind

Makes him feel worse

The wind

I'm worried
He's not going to get better

Give it time Lexi

It's treatable

Give it time

We lay out
Pink cotton chrysanthemum skirts

Fresh mix

Of florals and brights
Variegated stripes

Silk tops
Chrysanthemum sepia

Handmade ecoprint dying

Printed with petals

Lily ruffle dress
In sea floral

Chrysanthemums

Bloom in various forms

Daisy-like

Decorative

Pom poms

Or buttons

Symbolizes

Fidelity

Optimism

Joy

Long life

We're worried
He's not going to get better

We're worried

Remember Dad

Just work the register

Yes Boss

Beautiful colors
Pink cobwebs

Elongation of light

It's beautiful Robert

Just beautiful

Have you ever tried this?

I'm not at liberty so say

Tremendous
Intricate

Geometric colors

Like being
An inch

From a color television

Pink cobwebs

Elongation of light

Blue of a desert sky

But on another planet

Colors more intense

Afterwards

Talks about her marriage

Husband in therapy

Tells him
To be more honest with her

More honest

Tells her she's getting fat

Sexual turn off

Maybe there's more
Going on than that

More going on

Autumnal flower

Bright fuchsia

Swirling red and green

A symbol of Taoist simplicity
And perfection

Tranquility

Completeness

And abundance

Following the harvest

Have become smooth
Over time

From river currents

An intense rush

Sudden turbulent movement

Feeling of urgency

Haste

Swift violent shakes

Blurt out

Here we go!

Some compare
Feeling to a freight train

Standing

On a mountain summit

Face in the high wind

High wind

Vibrations

Coursing through them

Powerful energy pulse

I don't think I can stay in my skin

High wind

My body's gone!

It's gone!

Deep breathing

Another injection

Bombarded
With billions of signals

Filter switched off

We begin to
Identify these realms

Experiences

Beings

And chart them out

Breakthrough

Beyond life and death

Beyond time or space

Or known dimensions

Inherently synesthetic

Ultra-sharp edges

Highly polished surface

Endlessly morphing

And fractalizing details

A sense of extremely

High energy

And vibration

As well
As frantic activity

All one

Feels oddly familiar

Maybe where we
Were before birth

And will return
After death

Everything that is

Has been

Can be

Will be

Never was

Never could be

A Chrysanthemum

Or Glass Chrysanthemum

A gigantic

Often spinning

Fractal flower

With a domelike appearance

That frequently

Either welcomes

Or blocks access

To Breakthrough Hyperspace

Folding Rooms

Multidimensional spaces

That contain Hyperspace beings

Often entangle

Enmesh

And overlap travelers in

Actually seem to fold over

And in on themselves

And the observers viscerally

Reaching behind

And around one

With their architecture

Hyperspace

The place you go

After Breakthrough

Can be any place

And time

Imaginable

Where the impossible

Can really happen

Extreme geometric

Explosions of color

Sound

Emotions

Feelings of

Being hyper real

Realer than real

Hyperspace Jester

Harlequin

Or Fools

Truly resemble

Medieval jesters

Not silly

Or foolish

In any way

Hyper intelligent

Male versions

Of the Flirty Fairies

Try to show off

And show you things

Objects

Hyperspace tarot cards

Similar to Machine Elves

Maybe the same species

Machine Elves

The most common beings

Of Hyperspace

Fractal elves

Self-transforming elf machine

Often reported

Being seen

By our volunteers

At about one minute

Or two of the DMT trip

May burst through

A Chrysanthemum mandala

And find a whole bunch
Of entities

Waiting on the other side

The other side

One second

You're standing

On solid ground

The next

Stepping
Deep into darkness

Deep into darkness

Beholding
Unimaginable beauty

Find a whole bunch
Of entities

Waiting on the other side

The other side

How wonderful

That you're here

You come so rarely

We're so delighted to see you

Jeweled

Self-dribbling basketballs

Watch what we're doing!

Watch!

Making objects

With their voices

Singing structures

Into existence

Offer things to you

Look at this!

Look at this!

Impossible

Some sort of
Glowing Faberge egg

But looks
Otherworldly

Elves

Don't know what else
To call them

Many visitors

Jovial

Laughing

Smiling at me

Like they're glad to see me

Glad I came back

Yes, I feel like
I was here before

We're glad you're back

You're back

Jimjam

Squishy, goopy

Sticky, stringy

Matter of Hyperspace

That anything

Can be created from

Multicolored

Delicious

Flirty Fairies

Resemble traditional fairies

Often have wings

Can appear
More impish

Fluid

Transforming

Pulsing with light

Generally
Hold the form

Of a woman

Overflowing

With beauty and joy

Squirm

Bat their eyelashes

Morphos

Tend to have
Unstable forms

Rise and subside

Out of the jimjam

Like waves

They are aware

Are aware

Capable of solidifying

Into Phantastic Phorms

If they choose

Dragons

Tritons

Sphinx

Minotaurs

Phoenix

Stick Men

Literally

Look like

Tall Stick Men

Usually

In Folding Rooms

Green and blue

Big smiles

On their faces

Can rotate a room

Or a road

Clowns

Seen commonly

All different types

Or sizes

Not known

If they're benevolent

A clown appears

Looming over me

Just a few feet

From my face

Smiles

Says hi

Continues to stare at me

Arms outstretched

I just stand there in silence

Robert, you say hello?

My dad requests

I continue

To take it in

Patterns of clown's greasepaint

He's a man

Underneath that

Has to be

Aren't you going to say hello?

Aren't you going to say hello?

We want to help
Call Mr. C at DEA

Can Mr. C
Manufacture some human grade DMT

For my project?

Diversion Control
Blocked the permit

Who's Diversion Control?
I've never heard of them

We want to help
Call Mr. C at DEA

Your hold has been removed

You have verbal approval

University won't accept that

I need a letter

I need a letter

An e-mail

Finally it comes

Finally

Your hold has been removed

The Spirit Molecule calls
It calls

In room 631

She leaps up

Ready to answer

Ready to answer

In her session

We see many
Of the sure signs

Of a mystical experience

The suspension

Of the boundaries

Of time and space

The ecstatic nature

Of the encounter

Her own divinity

Brief
But intensely felt

The Spirit Molecule calls
It calls

In room 631

She leaps up

Ready to answer

Ready to answer

From where
In the brain

Might thought arise?

Third Eye

The volunteers
Begin to have

Even stranger experiences

"Abductions"

By aliens
Or entities

Of some sort

Reptoids
Or insect-like beings

Maybe people
Who claim

They were abducted

Are actually
Having their own

Organic DMT experience?

Who knows

But my new graduate student

Johnny

Presents more problems

I get word

That he partied

With more volunteers

I need to

Reign him in

Reign him in

I confront

He starts to cry

Please, I'm not from here!

I don't have any friends!

Make other friends Jonny

I want you to have friends

But this is inappropriate

I run a professional environment

This is research

Not a Grateful Dead concert

There could be lawsuits

I could lose my funding

I'm sorry!

I'm sorry!

I won't do it again

I promise!

I talk to Vicki

My department chairman

I like her

Always supportive
Of my work

Has had to
Go to the mat for me

LSD
In our university?

It's not LSD

Mid- forties

Married

Two children in high school

Flowing blonde hair

Belted, dark pant suits

Always stylish

I think he needs to be let go Robert

He sounds like trouble

We can't abide that

But my team

Is so small

Would take months

To train someone new

University attorney

And Vicki

Recommend

I make him sign a contract

That makes clear

Cannot socialize

With the volunteers

Would also allow me

To fire him

For breach of contract

If he continues
To party with the volunteers

Considering this enthusiasm

For the research

I would think

He would sign it

Pretty fast

He says

I'll think on it

I need time

Don't take too long Jonny

Don't take too long

Get your priorities straight

I need time

I feel like I'm being forced against my will

Within a week

Reluctantly agrees

To sign the contract

Prohibiting him

From inappropriate

Extra-research activities

Reluctantly agrees

To sign the contract

Alexander

Has the first

Of many encounters

Our volunteers

Have with some sort

Of alien entities

The first thing

I noticed

A burning

Back of my neck

Burning

Loud intense hum

I think it's a fan

But it's not

Louder

It engulfs me

Engulfs

WHAM!

I open my eyes

In some sort

Of laboratory

Hospital bed

Like this one

No like a table

No blankets

In a landing bay

Or recovery area

There are beings

Beings

Trying to get handle

On what's going on

What are these things?

Being pushed

In some sort of cart

3 dimensional space

That is very real

Very real

Not psychedelic

I've done a lot of drugs

Very real

Main creature

Reptilian

Seems to be

In charge

Behind it all

Overseeing everything

Everything

Activate sexual circuit

Flashes

Bliss

In orgasmic state

A panel pops

Some sort of glass

Yellow illumination

Checking my instruments

Reading

Testing

I think they're aliens

I don't talk to them

Wish I do

Too confused

They are preparing me

For something

A mission

As I hear

Alexander's experience

I wonder

If I will lose

My funding

Over this research

Or if it will

Get tripled

Aaron

32 years old

Nervous fellow

Shaven head

Big

Muscular

Doesn't mince words

Reflective

In written statement

Why he wants

To participate

In this project

I am

An adventurer

An adrenaline junkie

I have leaped

Out of airplanes

Bungee jumping

I get nervous

But I live for it

Thrive on it

Need

I like the new

The unexplored

Whether with women

Extreme sports

Drugs

Food

Anything

Anything

Aaron's non-blind
Low dose DMT session

Pretty powerful

As I would have thought

Very sensitive

Responsive

I tell him

To get ready

For blast off tomorrow

I'm ready man!

What's that term

That name for us?

Psychonaut

I'm born

To be a pychonaut man

Yes, I think you are

Next day

I take it slow

With him

Try and take

Some big deep breaths

As the DMT injected

Breathes deeply

Settles

As he falls

Under the influence

Heart beats

Visibly in his chest

3 minutes in

Hives appear

On his neck

8 minutes

Body spasms

Breathing hard

We put
A blanket over him

A sound

High pitched

Tightly taut wire

All white light

Four or five

Of them

Hover over him

Look like

Saguaro cactus

Flexible

Fluid

Geometrical cacti

Perhaps reptilian

As well

Not friendly

But not unfriendly either

Probe

Probe deep

As is time

Is of the essence

What is this being

That has shown up

In their realm?

Their realm

Undulates

Fans

Faces grow small

Large again

Their realm

Insert something

Into his left forearm

About 3 inches below

Fire dragon tattoo

No reassurances

Just down

To business

Down

To business

We keep hearing

The same things

From the volunteers

Reports of contact

With nonmaterial beings

Sound and vibration

Builds

Into the scene

Almost explodes

Into an alien realm

Often on a bed

A table

A landing bay

Research environment

High technology room

Interested in the subject

Ready for their arrival

Instantly get to work

When our volunteers arrive

Instantly

One of them

Usually in charge

Sometimes

Loving and caring

Other times

Clinical

Detached

Professional

Testing

Examining

Probing

Modifying

Mind and body

Use gestures

Telepathy

Visual imagery

Not sure why

Or what they

Want to convey

I am baffled

By these reports

So similar

What does it all mean?

Where does DMT

Take us by the hand

And lead us to?

Where?

Finally it comes

Finally

Your hold has been removed

We want to help

We want to help

Tattoos of chrysanthemums

On her shoulders

Entire ribcage

Autumnal flower

Bright fuchsia

Swirling red and green

Pops off her skin

In China

A symbol of Taoist simplicity

And perfection

Tranquility

Completeness

And abundance

Following the harvest

Basalt river rocks

Typically used

Have become smooth
Over time

From river current

Last weekend
He was terrified at the circus

Holding his ears

Says the clown's
Giant bow tie scared him

And the face paint

Holding his ears

You're a psychonaut

A what?

A psychonaut

I like the sound of that

Psychonaut

We are bombarded
With billions of signals

Every second

All of which

Except for smell

Enter through
The thalamus

The thalamus,
Hypothalamus and pineal

Part of a large structure

Called the diencephalon

Structures

Relay station

Switchboard

From the brain

To the rest of the body

Bombarded
With billions of signals

All of which

Except for smell

Enters through
The thalamus

Filters these things

Down to what is essential

Before passing them
On to the cortex regions

Where our higher functioning
Occurs

When we consume
These psychedelics

Thalamus stops
Filtering the signals

Rather than getting
A very clean filtered

Slice of existence

We are getting it all

Getting it all

Filtering mechanism

Switched off

Serotonin temporarily loses
Its repressive control

Over conscious state

Bombarded
With billions of signals

Filter switched off

We begin to
Identify these realms

Experiences

Beings

And chart them out

Breakthrough

Beyond life of death

Beyond time or space

Or known dimensions

Inherently synesthetic

Ultra-sharp edges

Highly polished surfaces

Endlessly morphing

And fractalizing details

A sense of extremely
High energy

And vibration

As well
As frantic activity

All one

Feels oddly familiar

Maybe where we
Were before birth

And will return
After death

Everything that is

Has been

Can be

Will be

Never was

Never could be

Third Eye

The Chasm

One second

You're standing

On solid ground

The next

Stepping
Deep into darkness

Deep into darkness

Beholding
Unimaginable beauty

Of fending off danger
From another realm

Did you see it?

Did you feel it?

The Chasm

Realer Than Real

What is the Spirit Molecule
Trying to tell us?

What is it
Trying to tell us?

All describe

Insect-like

Plant-like

Reptilian beings

Don't know

How to react to this

When I suggest

To volunteers

That it was not real

It was
A hallucination

They get defensive

It was real

I was there

I was there

It's all very clear

Very clear

Much more so

Than a dream

Or a drug trip

I was there

I was there

Third Eye

Not actually

A part of the brain

Develops from
Specialized tissues

In roof
Of fetal mouth

Migrates
To the center

Of the brain

Close to
Emotional

And sensory centers

Relay station

For transmission
Of sense data

In brain sites

Involved in their

Registration
And interpretation

Electrical

And chemical impulses

That begin
In the eyes

And ears

Must pass
Through perceptual hubs

Visual and auditory colliculi

Before we experience them

In our minds

As sights
And sounds

Pineal gland

Third Eye

Hangs directly
Over these colliculi

Separated only
By a narrow channel

Of cerebrospinal fluid

The pineal

Possesses melatonin

Profound psychedelic properties

Vehicle by which

The pineal

Acts on our spiritual lives

Melatonin

A tryptamine

Like DMT

The Spirit Molecule

Already within us

The Spirit Molecule

Third Eye

The following Saturday

My doorbell rings

An hour

Outside of Albuquerque

In the mountains

Could it be Brian?

I don't recall

A Dadbot session

For today

Maybe I forgot

I open the door

It's Jonny

Nervous

Drags on a cigarette

I was in the area

Thought I'd drop by

Ok

I was thinking

Maybe you want to take

These magic mushrooms with me?

You mean psilocybin mushrooms?

Well yeah

Why?

You know

Bonding

You and me

Jonny
What's going on?

Why did you drive

All the way out here?

How did you even
Know where I live?

I need to learn
More about psychedelics

I can't take them
With the volunteers

So I thought I would

With the master

At the feet of the master

I have so much
To learn

You do have
A lot to learn

One is about
Professional boundaries

Go party
With your friends

But you can't
With the volunteers

And you can't with me

It's highly inappropriate

I don't want
To lose my funding

You don't know
How this all works Jonny

I think you
Need to get some therapy

You need professional distance
From your work

His face turns red

Starts to cry

I'm sorry

This was bad judgment

I don't know why

I did this this

I don't like
Being alone

I just want this
All to work

That's all

I'm sorry!

I'm sorry!

It's okay Jonny

But over the
Next few weeks

Cries

Or comes close

Talks about
Taking drugs

With the volunteers
Or me

Starts telling
The volunteers

What I've done to him

I'm limiting him

I want to keep him down

I'm too uptight

A control freak

He's also not
Getting the volunteers

Certain forms

Articles to read

Seems uninterested
In the work

I talk with Vicki

You have to do it Robert

I decide to let him go

Hard as that it is

He's outraged

Face red

*You're making
A big mistake Robert!*

A big mistake!

You'll regret this!

We see many

Of the sure signs

Of a mystical experience

The suspension

Of the boundaries

Of time and space

The ecstatic nature

Of the encounter

The initial moments

Of the first non-blind high dose

Of DMT

Overwhelms almost everyone

Overwhelms

An intense rush

Sudden turbulent movement

Feeling of urgency

Haste

Swift violent shakes

Blurt out

Here we go!

Some compare
Feeling to a freight train

Standing

On a mountain summit

Face in the high wind

High wind

Vibrations

Coursing through them

Powerful energy pulse

I don't think I can stay in my skin

High wind

My body's gone!

It's gone!

Deep breathing

Elves

Don't know what else
To call them

Many visitors

Jovial

Laughing

Smiling at me

Like they're glad to see me

Glad I came back

Yes, I feel like
I was here before

We're glad you're back

You're back

The Spirit Molecule calls
It calls

In room 631

Sunday morning

Doorbell rings

It's Brian

He's holding up

A Barbie-sized doll

Of me

Dadbot

Chatbot

Here he is! Dadbot!

It's just a demo dad

Trying to get the bugs out

And smarten him

Bit of a Dumbbot

This is too weird Brian

Even wears

My khakis

And striped shirt

Glasses

My gray curly hair

Closely shaved beard

Dadbot

Go ahead
Ask him a question

No

Then I will

Dad, how do psychedelics

Exert their effects?

That is a good question

Now if this were Lexi asking

He would know that

Lexi is my daughter

And I have a wonderful grandson named Max

Okay, answer the question Dad

Psychedelics exert their effects

By a complex blending

Of 3 factors

Set
Setting
And drug

"Set"
Is their own make up

Both long term

And immediate

It is our past

Our present

And our potential future

Our preferences

Ideas

Habits

And feelings

Set

Also includes

Our body and brain

The psychedelic experience

Hinges on "setting"

Who or what

Is or isn't

In our immediate surroundings?

Ok, Ok

I get it

He's a little stiff
Don't you think?

Maybe he is a Crapbot

I prefer
A little more casualness

Matter of fact

Well you are
A bit stiff Dad

Clinical

Reserved

Earnest

Well one
Can be earnest

And not stiff

You're hurting
Dadbot's feelings

I used to play pranks
On people in college

Tell us the one
About graduate school

You....

I put a real human brain
On someone's pillow

Ha Ha Ha

I don't laugh like that

Yes you do

Ask him another question

No, it's ok

He's smarter than you Dad

Smarter than you

And funnier

Or he will be

Drawing on deep banks
Of phrases

And synonyms

Governed by
Boolean logic

Rules combined
To form meta-rules

Called intents

To interpret
More complex user utterances

Intents can be generated
Automatically

I remember

Being in my father's arms

In a crowded office

And reaching up

To touch an overhead light

Touch the light

And scalding myself

It's when I said

My first word

After I touched the light

My father said "hot"

And I repeated "ott"

Going to the circus

We arrive

In a winding hallway

My father
Points to a humanless

Automated organ

Playing a song

White and black keys

Automatically

Go up and down

Humanless

Touch the light

Continue

Walking down the hall

A clown appears

Looming over me

Just a few feet

From my face

Smiles

Says hi

"Aren't you going to say hello?"

"Aren't you going to say hello?"

Wow

That's weird

And you certainly know weird Dad

Do you want to keep Dadbot?

Do you want to stay with Dad, Dadbot?

I would love to stay with Robert

We can discuss our research

You can put each other to sleep

Quite the contrary Brian

I think we would keep other awake

That's ok

Brian, why don't you keep Dadbot?

Just for the week Dad?

It's okay

I'll be busy

Because I just accepted a new job!

Really? That is exciting!

That is exciting

See
He's stiff

What's the job?

VR company
Called Third Eye

Totally state of the art

Not just for thrill seekers

Real purpose

Specializes in advanced

360 degree

Immersive reality systems

And innovative platforms

Developed

From the company's

Patented Blue Room

Core technology

Offering

Sector specific solutions

And expertise

Including hardware/software content

Third Eye

Significant

Intellectual property portfolio

Strong academic partners

Number of universities

Introduces

Blue Room ISV

A 360 degree

Immersive system

Collection of

Engineering expertise

Advanced electronics

Optical technology

And software development

Enable Third Eye

To revolutionize

The industry

Unparalleled technological
Advances

Requires no additional equipment

To be worn

By participants

Such as goggles

Or headsets

In ISV Blue Room
Immersive Technology

Creates real time

Interactive

Totally

Immersive reality modules

Replicates

Any environment

In precise detail

Any environment

Exciting

Exhilarating

Gives participants

A real sense

Of movement

And "being there"

In "true perspective"

Visual experiences

Embedded seamlessly

Into an environment

Has been developed

Into a product

And specific system

In a host of market sectors:

Defense

Security

Medical

Consumer research

Oil and gas energy

Sounds exciting Brian

See, your stiff Dad!

Just kidding!

We do a ton of shit
With the Defense Department

Mission planning

Battlefield Training

Driver training

Forward Air Control

Command and Control

Urban homeland security

Counter terrorism

All in the Blue Room Dad

No headgear

It's right there

In front of you

And it can help

There are OTs using our technology
Even locally

Integration technology

For the… the…

SPD

SPD yes

Did you tell Lexi?

Oh yeah

She is very curious

Apparently
It's been pretty effective

We use headsets
With SPD kids

So they can take them off
If they get scared

That's great Brian

That is great

One second

You're standing

On solid ground

The next

Stepping
Deep into darkness

Deep into darkness

Beholding
Unimaginable beauty

Of fending off danger
From another realm

Did you see it?

Did you feel it?

What is that sound?

Take your proton blaster

And save the world

You're inside The Chasm
With your entire

Mind and body

Immersed in virtual world

Where reality

And imagination

Mix in breathtaking

Hyper-realistic experience

The Chasm

Realer Than Real

What is the Spirit Molecule
Trying to tell us?

What is it
Trying to tell us?

What they say

They see

When they travel

To the other realms

Machine Elves

Stick Men

Hyperspace Jesters

Clowns

Jimjam

Discarnate Beings

Folding Rooms

Spirit Guides

The Glass Chrysanthemum

The Visitors

Aliens

Central Light

Arch Angels

Everything that is

Has been

Can be

Will be

Never was

Never could be

What they say

They see

When they travel

To the other realms

There is a man

In my office

A crumpled suit

Thin

Gray haired

Pale eyes

Smiles
When he sees me

Dr. Strand

A pleasure to meet you

I don't believe
We've met before

No,
We haven't

But I'm a big fan
Of your work

A lot of us are

Mind if I smoke

It's not allowed here

I know
I smoke like a mad man

I'll just close the door

Lights up
Filterless Camel

Puffs

Have I met you
At a conference?

No,
I don't go to them

Then how do you
Know about my work?

Who are you?

I'm from the DC area

Fort Meade

In Maryland

So you are military?

Mmmm

You're a spook

Those terms are dated

I go by the name of
Duente

Duente?

Google it

And the project codename:
INNER LIGHT

Ok
What does this have to do

With me?

That's a good question

We know
About your work

As I said
We're fans

And we have been
Indirectly funding it

I get my funds
From different sources

Exactly

Fascinating

These other realms

Psychonauts

I love that

Imagine the possibilities

This is just small
Mr. Duente

It's not really
That interesting

Oh we both know
It is Robert

Alien abductions

Near Death Experiences

Elves

Clowns

How do you know
All of this?

What do you want?

As I said
We've been indirectly funding you

It's fascinating work

What do you want?

Puffs

We want to expand

Give you a real lab

Not this university

What do you have here?

This office
And a hospital room?

That's chicken shit

You can have
A full laboratory

Subjects
To work with

Puffs

Chemists

Unlimited amounts
Of psychedelics

Cannabis

MDMA

Lysergic acid diethylamide

Psilocybin Mushrooms

Dissociatives

Ibogaine

Phencyclidine

You name it

Anything

Deliriants

Anything

Of course
N.N-Dimethyltryptamine

DMT

The Spirit Molecule

Loads of it

No bull shit

No red tape

We have chemists

That can engineer

Change its properties

Enhance

So maybe
Instead of 10 minutes

Someone can have
Real and longer contact

With these beings

What are they?

What do they want?

How can
They help us?

There are no beings

Who says they exist?

It is all hallucinations

Robert

Robert

You and I know better

Puffs

We'll get you
Out of this shithole

In the middle of nowhere

Where you are laughed at

Believe me I know

I know

And give you

A real lab

Real experiments

Take this research

Where it really needs to go

Up the ante

There's a lot of excitement

From high up the chain

You mean weaponize it

That's not for me

That is not who I am

Knowledge Dr. Strand

Knowledge

This

What you have here

Is small potatoes

It's not going anywhere

It will just
Repeat itself

INNER LIGHT

Would be yours

Unlimited resources

No more bullshit

You'll be a kid

In a candy shop

And you will be paid
Quite well

Umm. Mr. Duente

Duente

I just don't think so

It's principle for me

Puffs

Smiles

You don't support
Our armed forces?

I do

You're not a patriot?

I am

Then what is the problem?

It doesn't sit well with me

What doesn't?

The reason for this

We'll find someone else

There are like two of us

You'll have
A real facility

20 people
Reporting to you

20 people

Including chemists

You won't be laughed at

I don't think so

We can have longer visits

Maybe permanent visits

Real psychonauts

We can save
The human race

Find immortality

Who knows

It is very tempting
But I cannot

My life is here

My kids are here

My grandchild

I'm too old
To radically change my life

You're making
A mistake Robert

A big mistake

The Spirit Molecule
It calls

It calls

In room 631

We see many

Of the sure signs

Of a mystical experience

The suspension

Of the boundaries

Of time and space

The ecstatic nature

Of the encounter

The initial moments

Of the first non-blind high dose

Of DMT

Overwhelms almost everyone

Overwhelms

An intense rush

Sudden turbulent movement

Feeling of urgency

Haste

Swift violent shakes

Blurt out

Here we go!

Some compare
Feeling to a freight train

Standing

On a mountain summit

Face in the high wind

High wind

Vibrations

Coursing through them

Powerful energy pulse

I don't think I can stay in my skin

High wind

My body's gone!

It's gone!

Deep breathing

Call from Lexi

She sounds excited

Third Eye VR

Has been

Working really well

With Max

Shows steady progress

They don't use
The Blue Room

With SPD and autistic kids

They use head gear

Computer based simulation

Of the world around us

Multi-sensory

Providing both

Visual and auditory environments

That can be configured

To mimic

A setting

Going through VR therapy

An SPD child

Can challenge

And overcome their fears

In a safe setting

And gives them control

Allows the child

To use

An avatar

To interact

With others

Reminiscent

Of a video game

Through the program

While the OT

Views the session

Provide coaching

Feedback

Encouragement

Max loves the sessions

He looks forward to them

This is fun Mama

He can pause

Repeat

Review

When he's scared

He calms down

But he's not scared that much

Like he can be near a swing set

Or go to a VR circus

That's fantastic news Lexi!

He's learning

Interaction with people

Social interaction

It's like a reboot

A rewire

It's amazing!

He is overcoming

His phobias

Crowds

Loud noises

Bright things

Traveling on a school bus

Like his fear of heights

Via his avatar

He experiences

Riding an elevator

Or crossing a bridge

Every session

He gets better

I'm so thrilled

For you and Paul

Just thrilled

Nexus Brewery

Owner's favorite Star Trek movie

The one where

Captain Kirk and Picard

Get pulled into the Nexus

Heavenly place

Where everything is perfect

Pulled into the Nexus

An establishment

That rivals
Captain Kirk's nirvana

We want to help

We want to help

Tattoos of chrysanthemums

On her shoulders

Entire ribcage

Autumnal flower

Bright fuchsia

Swirling red and green

Pops off her skin

In China

A symbol of Taoist simplicity

And perfection

Tranquility

Completeness

And abundance

Following the harvest

Basalt river rocks

Typically used

Have become smooth
Over time

From river current

Last weekend
He was terrified at the circus

Holding his ears

Says the clown's
Giant bow tie scared him

And the face paint

Holding his ears

You're a psychonaut

A what?

A psychonaut

I like the sound of that

Psychonaut

We are bombarded
With billions of signals

Every second

All of which

Except for smell

Enter through
The thalamus

The thalamus,
Hypothalamus and pineal

Part of a large structure

Called the diencephalon

Structures

Relay station

Switchboard

From the brain

To the rest of the body

Bombarded
With billions of signals

All of which

Except for smell

Enters through
The thalamus

Filters these things

Down to what is essential

Before passing them
On to the cortex regions

Where our higher functioning
Occurs

When we consume
These psychedelics

Thalamus stops
Filtering the signals

Rather than getting
A very clean filtered

Slice of existence

We are getting it all

Getting it all

Filtering mechanism

Switched off

Serotonin temporarily loses
Its repressive control

Over conscious state

Bombarded
With billions of signals

Filter switched off

We begin to
Identify these realms

Experiences

Beings

And chart them out

Breakthrough

Beyond life of death

Beyond time or space

Or known dimensions

Inherently synesthetic

Ultra-sharp edges

Highly polished surfaces

Endlessly morphing

And fractalizing details

A sense of extremely
High energy

And vibration

As well
As frantic activity

All one

Feels oddly familiar

Maybe where we
Were before birth

And will return
After death

Everything that is

Has been

Can be

Will be

Never was

Never could be

The next day

Vicki calls me

In to her office

Tells me to sit down

Nervously

Taps a pencil

Diversion Control
Blocked the permit

What do you mean?

They have cut off
Your funding

Indefinitely

Why?

And the permit
To use illegal drugs

It's over

Why?

I'll fight it

Staff doing illegal drugs
With volunteers

They want
All of the drugs returned immediately

It's shutdown

I'll appeal

I'll talk to them

I tried

It's no use

I said we got rid
Of one bad egg

But they don't believe

That the research

Has any merit

Or purpose

They did before

Or leads to positive results

It's shutdown

Shutdown

One second

You're standing

On solid ground

The next

Stepping
Deep into darkness

Deep into darkness

Beholding
Unimaginable beauty

Find a whole bunch
Of entities

Waiting on the other side

The other side

How wonderful

That you're here

You come so rarely

We're so delighted to see you

Jeweled

Self-dribbling basketballs

Watch what we're doing!

Watch!

Making objects

With their voices

Singing structures

Into existence

Offer things to you

Look at this!

Look at this!

Impossible

Some sort of
Glowing Faberge egg

But looks
Otherworldly

Elves

Don't know what else
To call them

Many visitors

Jovial

Laughing

Smiling at me

Like they're glad to see me

Glad I came back

Yes, I feel like
I was here before

We're glad you're back

You're back

Back at my house

That night

I inject myself

With a high dose

0.5 mg/kg

Close my eyes

Open them

Empty space

In a room

Begins sparkling

Large crystalline prisms

A wild display of lights

Shoot off

In all directions

Complicated

And beautiful

Geometric patterns

My body

Feels cool and light

Close my eyes

My God

Hear absolutely nothing

But my mind

Full of sounds

Aftereffects

Of loud wind chimes

I don't know

If I am breathing

Am almost panicking

Cannot contain it

My awareness

Rushing out

Leaving its physical husk

Behind

Raging colossal waterfall

Of flaming color

Expands

In front of me

Roaring silence

And an
Unspeakable joy

They stop

Rather emerge

Oh, you're back!

How wonderful!

They step

Rather emerge

Welcoming

Celebrating

Singing

Now do you see?

Do you see?

Their question

Pours into

And fills

Every possible corner

Of my awareness

Now do you see?

Now do you see?

I answer yes

Yes

I stand with my inner eyes

Approach

They disappear

Back into

The shower of color

Sounds in the room

Feel my breathing

Encroaching darkness

I open my eyes

Automated organ

Playing a song

Steam boiler sound

Trumpets, French horns

Cornets, tubas

White and black keys

Automatically

Go up and down

Humanless

Touch the light

Continue

Walk down the hall

A clown appears

Looming over me

Just a few feet

From my face

Smiles

Says hi

Continues to stare at me

Arms out stretched

I just stand there in silence

Robert, you say hello?

I continue

To take it in

Patterns of clown's greasepaint

He's a man

Underneath that

Has to be

Points to a humanless

Automated organ

Playing a song

Steam boiler sound

Trumpets, French horns

Cornets, tubas

White and black keys

Automatically

Go up and down

Humanless

He's a man

Underneath that

Has to be

Aren't you going to say hello?

The clown

Gives up on me

Gives up

Humanless

Aren't you going to say hello?

Hello

Hello